North Carolina

By Linda Crotta Brennan

Consultant
Nanci R. Vargus, Ed.D.
Primary Multiage Teacher
Decatur Township Schools, Indianapolis, Indiana

Children's Press®
A Division of Scholastic Inc.
New York Toronto London Auckland Sydney
Mexico City New Delhi Hong Kong
Danbury, Connecticut

Designer: Herman Adler Design
Photo Researcher: Caroline Anderson
The photo on the cover shows Looking Glass Rock during spring.

Library of Congress Cataloging-in-Publication Data

Brennan, Linda Crotta.
  North Carolina / by Linda Crotta Brennan.
    p. cm. — (Rookie read-about geography)
Includes index.
Summary: An introduction to North Carolina which focuses on the
state's geography.
  ISBN 0-516-22698-3 (lib. bdg.)   0-516-27822-3 (pbk.)
  1. North Carolina—Juvenile literature. 2. North Carolina—Geography—
Juvenile literature. [1. North Carolina.] I. Title. II. Series.
  F254.3 .B74 2003
  917.56—dc21   2002011537

JE
BRE
C ·2

CHILDREN'S PRESS, AND ROOKIE READ-ABOUT®,
and associated logos are trademarks and or registered trademarks
of Grolier Publishing Co., Inc. SCHOLASTIC and associated logos
are trademarks and or registered trademarks of Scholastic Inc.

1 2 3 4 5 6 7 8 9 10 R 12 11 10 09 08 07 06 05 04 03

Do you like the beach
and the mountains? Then
North Carolina is the state
for you!

North Carolina is in the southeast. Four states are next to North Carolina.

Virginia is to the north. Tennessee is to the west. Georgia and South Carolina are to the south. The Atlantic Ocean is to the east.

CANADA

WASHINGTON

OREGON

IDAHO

MONTANA

NORTH
DAKOTA

SOUTH
DAKOTA

WYOMING

NEBRASKA

NEVADA

UTAH

COLORADO

KANSAS

CALIFORNIA

ARIZONA

NEW MEXICO

OKLAHOMA

TEXAS

MINNESOTA

WISCONSIN

MICHIGAN

IOWA

ILLINOIS

INDIANA

OHIO

MISSOURI

KENTUCKY

ARKANSAS

TENNESSEE

MISSISSIPPI

ALABAMA

LOUISIANA

GEORGIA

FLORIDA

NEW HAMPSHIRE
VERMONT
MAINE

NEW YORK

MASSACHUSETTS
RHODE ISLAND
CONNECTICUT
NEW JERSEY
DELAWARE
MARYLAND

PENNSYLVANIA

WEST
VIRGINIA

VIRGINIA

Washington, D.C.

NORTH
CAROLINA

SOUTH
CAROLINA

ALASKA

CANADA

MEXICO

HAWAII

North

West

East

South

5

North Carolina has a
mild climate (KLYE-mit).
Weather that stays the
same most of the time is
called climate.

Charlotte

North Carolina has
beaches for swimming.
It has mountains to climb.
It also has forests, farms,
and cities.

Islands (EYE-luhndz)
line the coast of North
Carolina. They are called
the Outer Banks.

The first English
settlement was at
Roanoke (ROH-eh-nohk)
in the Outer Banks.

People fish off the Outer
Banks. Wild ponies run on
the islands.

4334 A

White Heron

There are also many birds
and sea turtles.

The land is low next to the coast. This is called the Coastal Plain. The Coastal Plain has rich soil.

Native Americans grew corn, beans, squash, and sunflowers there. Now, farmers grow tobacco, sweet potatoes, peanuts, corn, and soybeans.

Sweet potatoes

They raise chickens,
turkeys, and pigs.

West of the Coastal Plain
is the Piedmont Plateau
(PEED-mahnt pla-TOH).
This land is high and
mostly flat, like a table.
Another word for plateau
is tableland.

VIRGINIA

TENNESSEE

Piedmont Plateau

Raleigh

NORTH CAROLINA

Coastal Plains

North
West   East
South

SOUTH CAROLINA

GEORGIA

SCALE 1 inch = 100 miles

| 0 | Miles | 100 |

| 0 | Kilometers | 160 |

18

There are many factories in this part of North Carolina. Furniture, paper, and other things are made in these factories.

Many people live in
the Piedmont Plateau.
There are many jobs there.

Raleigh and six other big
cities are there. Raleigh is
the capital city of North
Carolina.

Raleigh

Western North Carolina has mountains. Mount Mitchell is the tallest. Sometimes there is snow on Mount Mitchell in the summer.

When the Cherokee (CHER-uh-kee) people were forced from their homes, many hid in these mountains. Many Cherokee still live there.

Bears, bobcats, and other animals live in the mountains. People like to hike, climb, and ski there.

North Carolina has beaches, mountains, forests, farms, and cities. Some people like to go rafting on the mountain streams.

There is something for everyone in North Carolina!

Words You Know

beach

Cherokee

Coastal Plain

factory

Mount Mitchell

Outer Banks

Raleigh

sweet potatoes

31

Index

About the Author

Before she could read, Linda Crotta Brennan created story cartoon strips. Now she writes both fiction and nonfiction for children. She also teaches writing and works at her local library in Rhode Island.

Photo Credits